I0345656

Thump

Thump

by Lisa Soland

Illustrations by Karah D. Tull

Text copyright © 2015 Lisa Soland
Illustrations copyright © 2015 Karah D. Tull

All rights reserved. No part of this publication may be reproduced, stored in a retrieval system, or transmitted in any form or by any means—electronic, mechanical, photocopy, recording, or other, except for brief quotations in written reviews, without the prior written permission of the publisher.

Climbing Angel Publishing
P.O. Box 32381
Knoxville, Tennessee 37930
http://www.ClimbingAngel.com

Manufactured in the United States of America
Book design by Zachary Hodges
Illustrations by Karah D. Tull

ISBN: 978-0-9965721-6-3
Library of Congress Control Number: 2016949837

This story is dedicated to Susan and her Bible study...

I was trying to write a book today, but I couldn't think of anything to write about.

Then I heard something in the other room.

It was an odd sound, like a soft

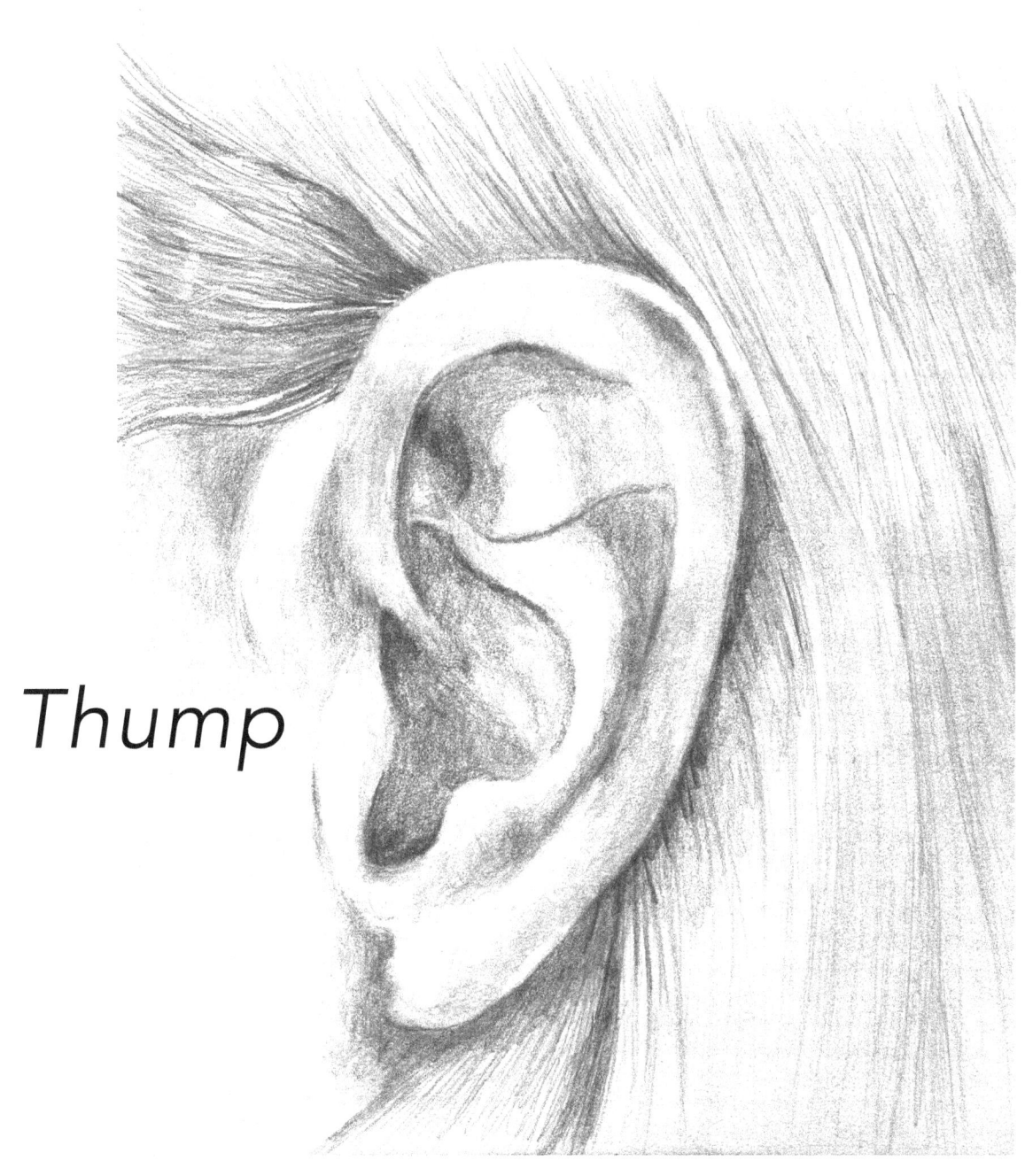

Thump

against a piece of glass.

It might have been a bird, I thought.

"Maybe a bird flew into our glass door."

I was afraid to look.

I didn't want to be right.

…and there lying on the ground, was the bird.

He looked
stunned
and
scared.

He was squawking.

I picked him up,
held him in my hands,

and began to pray.

"Dear God, please heal this bird. Make him whole again and help him to fly."

And the bird stopped squawking.

He looked up at me,
blinking his eyes,
open and shut,
and open and shut.

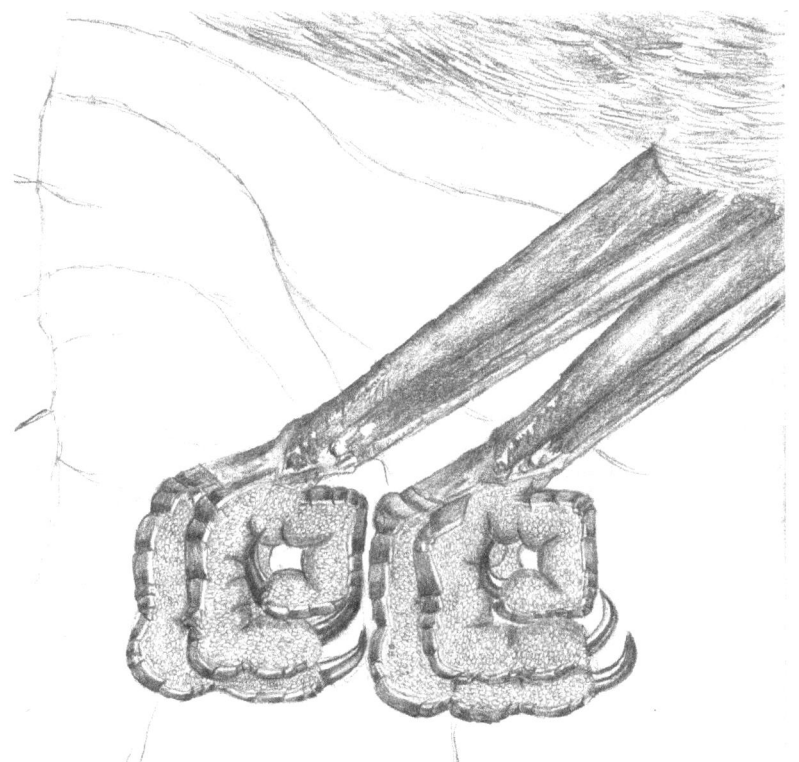

I noticed his little
legs curled up
tightly beneath him.

It didn't look
like anything
was broken.

"I know you're frightened,
but everything's going to be fine."

"Not one of you birds
can fall to the ground
without our heavenly Father
knowing about it."

Jesus
(Matthew 10:29)

Then I began to sing to the bird.

"I'll fly away,
O Glory.
I'll fly away."

"When I die
hallelujah
by and by,
I'll fly away."

I thought about all the times this bird had sung to me and to the sky and to the trees and to the entire neighborhood.

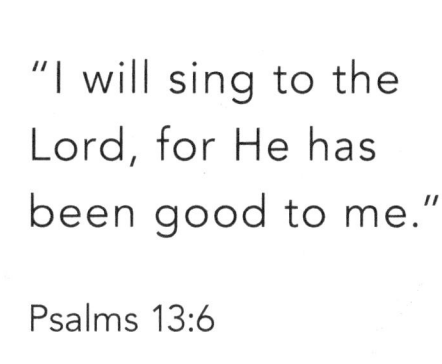

"I will sing to the Lord, for He has been good to me."

Psalms 13:6

The little bird seemed content in my hands, but I wanted him to finish getting better.

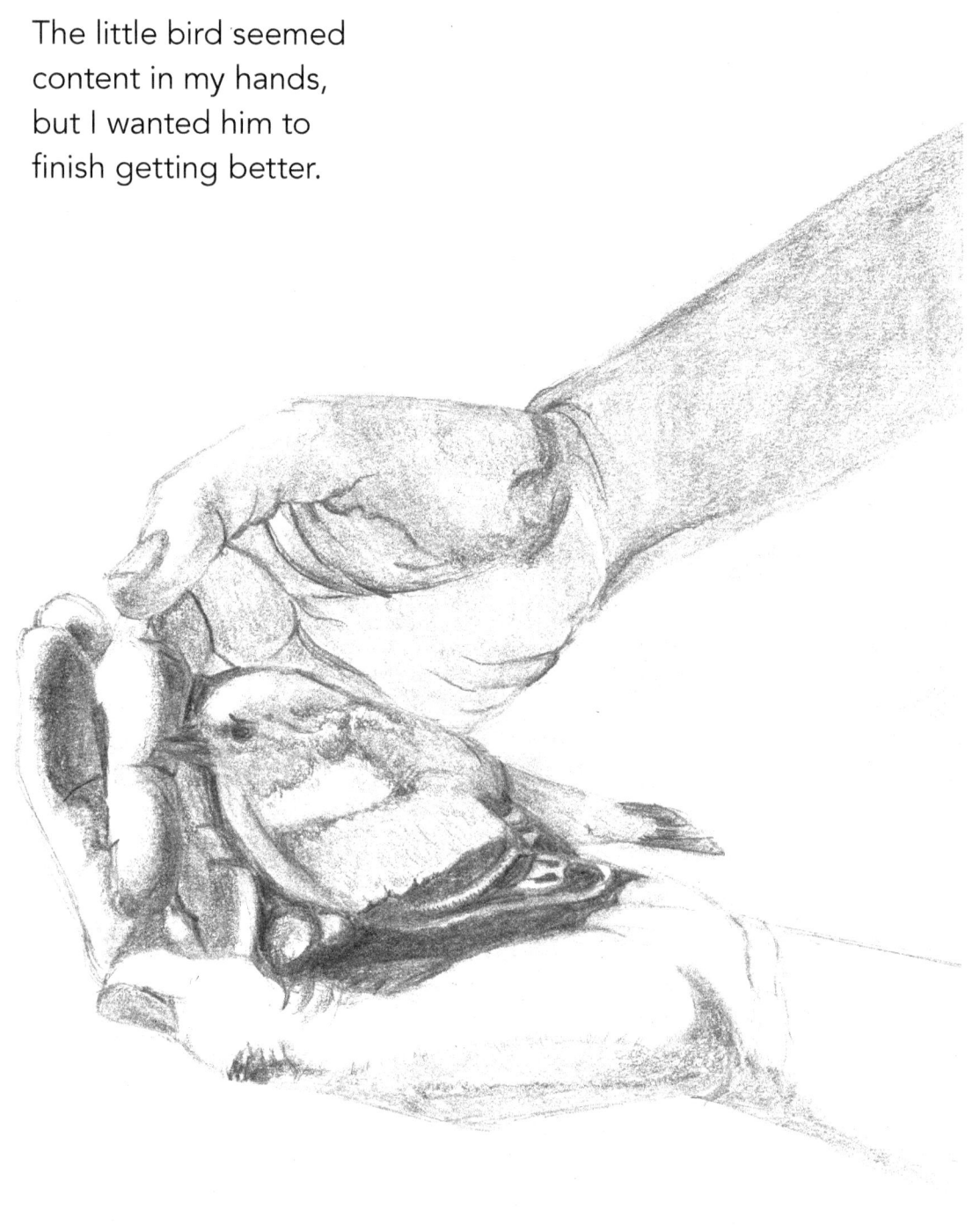

So, I carefully spread apart his claws and helped him to stand on my finger.

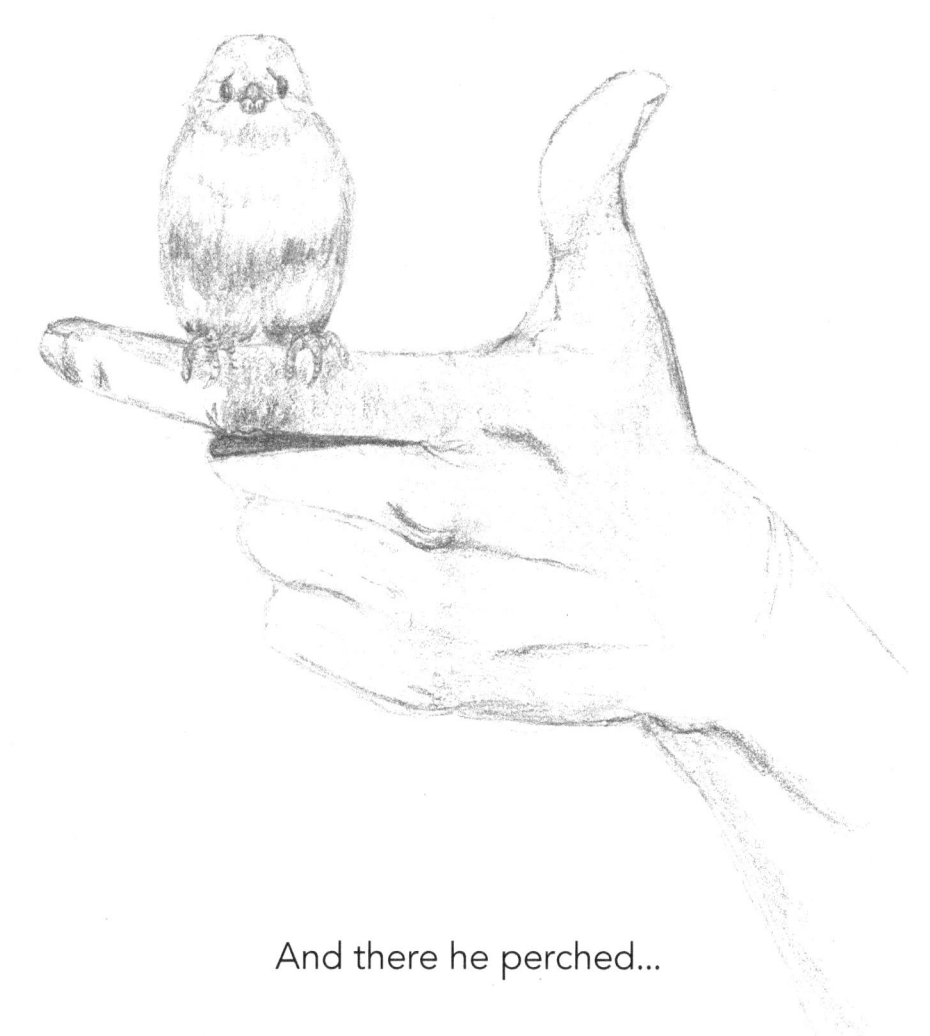

And there he perched...

And there he perched.

And there...

...he continued to perch.

"You're all better now, little bird.
You can fly away."

But he seemed perfectly happy
staying right where he was.
He climbed back down into
the palm of my hand.

I stroked his soft feathers.
It was amazing to pet a wild bird.

He was lovely.

I thought about keeping him, but the trees looked so very empty without him.

It was time for him to go home.

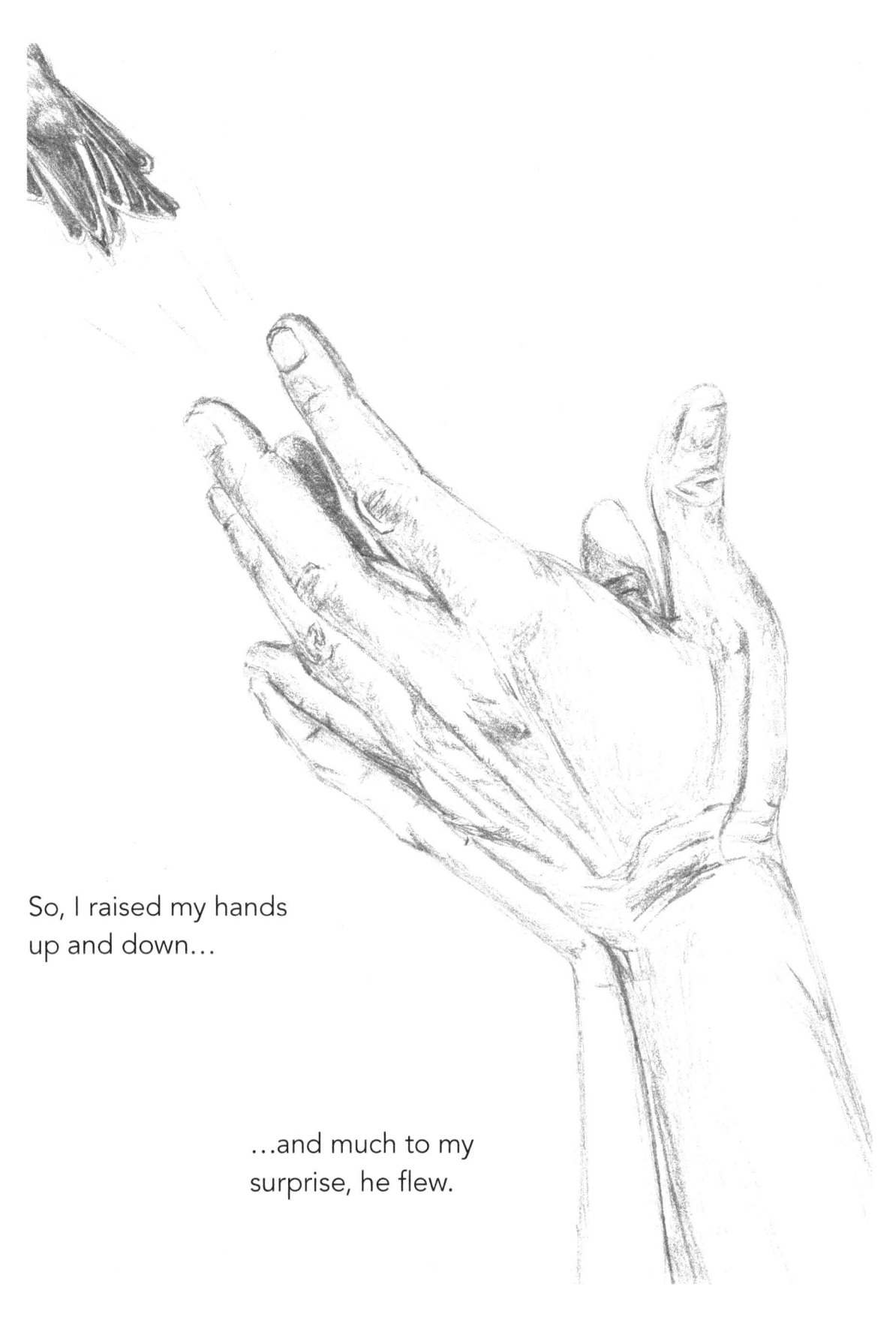

So, I raised my hands up and down...

...and much to my surprise, he flew.

Up,
Up,
and away he flew.

Above me, above the housetops, and into the beautiful clouds.

I asked God to protect him,
to keep him safe,
and to help him never fly
into the glass door again.

Then I had an idea.

"Birds never fly into other birds. I'll draw pictures of his friends, and hang the drawings on the glass door."

"That should work just fine!"

I returned to my desk
and tried again to write my book.
But I still couldn't think of anything to write about.

I *missed* my little bird.

Then it hit me.

"I'll write a book about how God,
through His loving grace and kindness, allowed me to watch
Him heal one of His beloved creatures."

And so I did.

Then I shared the book with people I didn't even know…

…and they enjoyed the story, too.

"Thank you God
for healing the little bird
and for helping me
to think of something
to write about."

Amen.

ABOUT CLIMBING ANGEL PUBLISHING

Climbing Angel Publishing exists for the purpose of sharing stories of hope and encouragement.

PHILIPPIANS 4:8
JEREMIAH 29:11

The following works are available from Climbing Angel Publishing at www.ClimbingAngel.com, Amazon.com, and major bookstores.

The Christmas Tree Angel
The Unmade Moose
Thump
Somebunny To Love

www.ingramcontent.com/pod-product-compliance
Lightning Source LLC
Chambersburg PA
CBHW061937290426
44113CB00025B/2937